[illegible]

Made in the USA
Columbia, SC
18 May 2022

60590329R00061